A Touch of Inspiration through Poems

LINDA GLASPER KING

ISBN 978-1-64569-507-3 (hardcover)
ISBN 978-1-64569-508-0 (digital)

Copyright © 2019 by Linda Glasper King

All rights reserved. No part of this publication may be reproduced, distributed, or transmitted in any form or by any means, including photocopying, recording, or other electronic or mechanical methods without the prior written permission of the publisher. For permission requests, solicit the publisher via the address below.

Christian Faith Publishing, Inc.
832 Park Avenue
Meadville, PA 16335
www.christianfaithpublishing.com

Printed in the United States of America

This Fine Christmas Morn

I awoke early this Christmas morn
And ran to our Christmas tree
I wanted to see all the Christmas gifts
Especially the ones for me

I looked beneath the glimmering tree
And saw a box all tattered and torn
Had someone forgotten to wrap this gift
On this fine Christmas morn

The tree had a shining star
And a twinkle in its lights
It reminded me that this was
A most special holy night

As I stood there gazing
At the beautiful Christmas tree
I heard joyous singing
And wondered who it could be

I ran to the window
But couldn't see a thing
Still I heard singing
Saying glory to the king

Then I heard a voice proclaim
That a savior had been born
To save a wretched world you see
On this fine Christmas morn

I looked again at the tattered box
And realized that this was me
And the birth of this newborn savior
Would truly set me free

I looked inside the tattered box
And all I saw was sin
This tattered box was telling me
That I had no peace within

Of all the gifts around this tree
None could ever compare
The gift God gave to this world
So full of trouble and despair

As you look beneath your Christmas tree
This fine Christmas morn
Are all your gifts neatly wrapped?
Or are they all tattered and torn.

Faithfulness

Behold the Lamb of God
How marvelous is his name
You are the living word
I will not complain

You have made it this far by faith
And you were never alone
You have that trusted assurance
Just tie a knot and hang on

Stir up the gift from God
Let your anointing fall on me
Guide my steps dear Lord
And lead me to Calvary

Lord, I am redeemed
And I know it was your blood
It was your grace and mercy
Lord that is love

Weeping maybe just for a night
And the battle will not be yours
You are my King of kings
And my Lord of lords

In the midnight hour of quietness
You can still away in the night
To say a little prayer to Jesus
Lord I want to do right

Lord, put a fence around me
For my troubles want last always
And the weapons formed for me will not prosper
Lord, you have my total praise

In your sanctuary, Lord
I will exhort your name on high
Give ear to me, Lord Jesus
In the sweet by and by

I have been there and done that
Can't nobody turn me around
Your love has lifted me up
High up from the ground

I don't always feel tired
I'm taking a day at a time
Lord, be my peace
And let my light so shine

Oh, how I want to see him
And just to see his face
For he will reign forever
In his holy place

He keeps his eyes on the sparrow
He has made away for me
Lord, you are the reason I made it over
And you are my testimony

I'm leaning on his merciful arms
Because he's sweet I know
Do not pass me by dear savior
If you send me, I will go

There is so much that I owe him
And I will surrender it all
For God gave his son
And his son paid it all

Whenever I need him the most
A blessing is in the storm
He comes to my rescue
To move away the thorns

I will be on his battlefield
And it's good for me to know
That I have a friend in Jesus
And I will never let him go

All my rain of blessings
My God surely did it
My Lord and Savior did it all
To him, I am committed

My God is a wonder
It is alright with my soul
For he is my solid rock
He's more than silver and gold

Some glorious morning
On a bright and shining day
I'll be flying on home
Up the King's airway

When that mighty ship from Zion
Set sail to yonder shore
I'll be at the glorious meeting
And time will be no more.

The Great Ocean Blue

Oh sea, oh sea, what powerful waves roll in
Longed to be controlled by the mightiest of men

The strong tides and currents that will not behave
Will send the greatest of men to a watery grave

The power you possess that man cannot control
The secrets you have kept since days of old

What magnificent treasures lie beneath your waves
The lives of soldiers and seamen and the African slaves

When storms are raging the fierce waves will attack
Capsizing ships from their chartered track

In the stillness of the night, you're as calm as can be
As the moon light glimmers from sea to sea

Your colorful waters of blue green and grey
That glistens in the hot sun's golden rays

You stand in command of all that floats
The ships, the tankers, and the rugged tug boats

You're a force of nature that cannot be tamed
You're the master of the waters that play no games.

It's a Man's Song

I must do right and do my part
To bring peace and joy to my lady's heart
I must do what a man should do
To do my best to take care of you
It's a man's song

I'm not doing anything wrong
Just finding a way to be more strong
Sometimes I need space to be
Just God and me, just God and me
It's a man's song

My mind is not gone
Sometimes I just want to be alone
To think about other ways
So there will be better days
It's just a man's song

You are my love
I thank God above
He sent me a mate
To love and not hate
It's a man's song

You are my love, my children's mother
Together we can depend on each other
I'll be there for you, and you'll be there for me
I need a little space to set my mind free
It's a man's song

Sometimes I need space
Just to stay in this race
To be that man whose saved by grace
Lord, help me to seek your holy face
It's just a man's song

We live in a day when so much is going on
Killings and stealing and broken up homes
These are times when we must stand together
To hold one another in stormy weather
It's a man's song

Don't put me in a corner and expect me to stand
I'm going to come out and stand as a man
I want to do right, just let me be free
Stand by my side and let me be me
It's a man's song

Don't cloud my mind with insecure feelings
I'm doing my best, I'm always willing
I will always love you, and you'll forever be mine
God brought us together in his perfect time
It's a man's song, just a man's song.

My Mommy

My Mommy loves me
She hugs me a lot
My Mommy loves me
Because I'm a little tot

My Mommy loves me
She tells me to be good
My Mommy loves me
When I don't do as I should

My Mommy loves me
No matter what I do or say
My Mommy loves me
That makes me feel okay

My Mommy loves me
When I'm sad and blue
My Mommy loves me
And I love her too

My Mommy loves me
She sends me to school
My Mommy loves me
Because I'm learning the golden rule

My Mommy loves me
She kisses me good night
My Mommy loves me
That makes me feel alright.

If I Could

If I could feed the world's hunger
And take all its hurt away
Then I can find the homeless some shelter
And give them a place to stay

If I could teach one child
That love can endure all things
That sometimes in this fragile life
We must suffer through some pain

If I could wipe away the teardrops
From the eyes of a mother's face
Or hug away the worries of a father
When a child has fallen from grace

If I could see the world
Through the eyes of a little child
Then I can see the innocence
And the sincerity of his smile

If I could help a brave soldier
In the uncertainty of a bloody war
Then I could bring him home again
To knock on his family's door

If I could gather all the people
And give them one big hug
Then I would tell them it is from God
And he's sending his everlasting love.

My Country and Me

I am an American
In this land of plenty and free
This land of opportunity
That was abundantly passed on to me

What does it mean to be an American
To stand proud with honor and grace
This land of opportunity
For every creed religion or race

This country stands proud and ready
To fight for what it believes
Ready to give aide and assistance
To those who are in great need

Our promising Lady Liberty
Standing taller than most trees
The stars and stripes of Old Glory
Blowing firmly in the breeze

The bald eagle flying high and mighty
A symbol of strength in this land
Makes you feel proud
Proud to be an American.

Help Me, Lord

Help me, Lord, to rise above my sins
Let your word abide deep within
Show me how to live for you
Show me, Lord, what I must do

Teach me, Lord, what I must say
Teach me, Lord, how I should pray
Give me, Lord, strength each day
Lead me, Lord, this vessel of clay

Help me, Lord, to forgive all men
Help me, Lord, to make amends
Give me rest for my weary soul
Give me, Lord, your hand to hold

Guide me, Lord, so I will not stray
Order my steps along the way
Comfort me, Lord, when I am sad
Keep me, Lord, when times are bad

Encourage me, Lord, when dreams fall through
Keep me, Lord, until I see you.

Night and Day

When night comes forth the day has gone
The stars shine bright all night long

A whisper of wind blows gently a breeze
A ripple of waves across the seas

The clouds move silently amid darken skies
The glisten moon prepares to rise

The hush hush silent that tiptoed through the night
Now burst with chatter from creature delight

The dawn of a new day quietly appears
While the red breasted robin sung joyous cheers

Flowers burst with color touch by the sun warm rays
Clothed in beauty for just a few days

As the evening draw nigh and all things still
The day prepares to rise over the eastly hill.

Coming Home to a Home

In this world are many places
some might call them home
Travelers often pass through this way
but now they are gone

The foundation of this home is strong
that's where your strength is found
For it is built on righteousness
and on solid ground

In the yard are flowers of every kind
the blessings you can receive
For God rains on the just and unjust
and whosoever believe

At the door is the welcome mat
and forgiveness beckons you in
It will not ask any questions
or care where you have been

The living room is where people are greeted
even angels might be entertained
God has no respecter of person
all are treated the same

The kitchen is the heart of the home
that's where love abides
Where the table is spread
and your cup runs over and flows down the sides

In the basement are the trials and tribulations
that you are going through
Where grace and mercy
has been given to you, you and you

The bathroom is where souls are washed
by the blood on a rugged cross
Where slates are wiped clean
and Jesus paid the cost

The bedrooms are the sleeping quarters
where the weary shall be at rest
From laboring in the vineyard
and doing your very best

What is a home without secret closets
where sincere prayers are said
Where petitions are laid before the Lord
by humble and bowed down heads

The attic is where the memories
of all life is played
Some call it heaven
for that's where treasures are laid

This home has an aroma
That's mighty sweet to smell
For the faithful who breathes upon it
is saved from a burning hell

Then there is the Master Builder
the creator and ruler of all things
For glory and honor shall be thine
for he is our King.

Light Over Darkness

God sent his only begotten son
To save mankind from sin
God saw the evil in this world
And how man was taking it in

Some were bloody murderers
And had no love in their hearts
Others were liars and thieves
And adulterers had a part

Idolaters they worshipped
The worldly things of this earth
The money the gold the silver
To our souls they had no worth

Fornicators lusting their way
And the deceitful doing evil in the dark
And woe the day will come
like when Noah went into the ark

They persecuted the righteous
And mocked the word of God
Death and damnation await them
Down the sinful road they trod

If only they would turn to God
And repent of their evil deeds
For God looks beyond our faults
To see all our needs

The Lamb of God was sacrificed
On Calvary's rugged cross
He shed His precious blood
So that mankind would not be lost.

God, Watch Over Me

As I move forward in life
Not knowing what I want to be
There are so many things I want to do
God, watch over me

Maybe I'll go to school and learn
Or get a college degree
Teach me all thy ways, Lord
And, God, watch over me

If I go into the military
And serve my country free
I'm a soldier in a foreign land
Please, God, watch over me

I must seek and explore opportunities
To help determine my destiny
To work diligently with discipline and perseverance
May God watch over me

God can unlock any door
When society wouldn't give me a key
Sometimes there are stumbling blocks
Please, God, watch over me

If I should fall along the way
Or stray too far from thee
Help me Lord to get back up
And, dear God, watch over me

If I come to a crossroad in life
My future I cannot see
I will kneel and pray for guidance
Please, God, watch over me

If I keep my soul anchored
Like a ship by a raging sea
My hopes my dreams my everything
Is in God, who watches over me.

Expressions of Love

A greeting card can say a lot of words
Flowers can show how we feel
A prayer can travel quickly to God
And with one touch He can heal

You can be sick for a little while
An illness can last a long time
Visits from friends and family
Can bring lots of bright sunshine

Kindness can lift someone's spirit
Encouragement can give you hope
Good friends can lend a helping hand
When life seems hard to cope

Smiles can show yourself friendly
And everyone has one to give
Laughter is medicine for the heart
We need it sometimes to live

Bestowing on someone the beauty of love
The time and patience to show that you care
Will make their day a day of rejoicing
To know that God is there.

Who Will I Send?

As I was in the beginning
The Word then and now
A preacher I am sending
Let me tell you how

I will send a man who is not perfect
But upright and just
I will send a man who is devoted
And in me he will trust

I will send a man who is able
To preach far and near
My words of salvation
To those who want to hear

I will send a man who is faithful
Steadfast and is strong
A man who will not waver between
What is right and what is wrong

I will send a man who is obedient
And will preach my word as it is
A man dedicated to serve me
My kingdom will be his

I will send a man who is humble and meek
Not boisterous nor is he proud
A man who will proclaim my word
In the streets or in a crowd

I will send a man who will lift me up
And exalt my name in praise
A man that will stand with me as his God
And serve me all his days

I will send a righteous man to lead my people
And teach them all my ways
A man who will stand on my promises
For I am his potter and he is my clay

A man is whose reflection I can see myself
Is a light in this ole world
It is the life he lives before men and women
And the little boys and girls

A man who will acknowledge me
Each day that he lives
A man who will seek my face
My wisdom I will give

I will send a man who will serve me
In good and difficult times
A man who will seek me still
For his heart is truly mine

A man to whom I will pour out my spirit
And my blessings are within his reach
A man who is not ashamed of my Gospel
A man who is ready to preach.

Journey through the Jungle

You heard the voice of the Father and you gave ear to His call
To preach the word of the gospel and preach to one and all
You stood at the gates of the jungle carrying the whole armor of God
And surly there was faith for the path you had to trod

As you journeyed through this jungle preaching as you go
The hyenas laughed and mocked you for the world is all they know
The elephants came charging to see what you are all about
In your mind was a vision in your heart you had no doubt

Lions roared with discouragement and faith they did lack
But, my Father God, you prayed, I will not turn back
The monkeys look down at you from high up in the trees
The God you serve sits higher and see your every need

The parakeets flying by telling their worldly views
You were called to preach the gospel to preach the divine good news
The serpent coil and slithering and they hiss at you in the night
You have a little talk with the Father and He makes everything alright

The cheetahs running fast after worldly ways to win
The race you said is not for the swift but to those who endure to the end
God walks with you he talks with you and he keeps you in his care
As you journey thru this jungle preaching sinners you better beware.

When Death Comes Knocking

When death comes knocking I will not be afraid
Because I have Christ and because I'm saved
When death comes knocking I'll just let him in
I've been washed in the blood I've been born again

Death has no power not even a sting
Jesus Christ is Lord, He's the King
Take my body but you can't touch my soul
My belief in Christ has made me whole

No death or hell can hold me down
When this ole body is laid in the ground
When I get to heaven it's the place to be
Because Jesus has said He'll be with me

Ready or not, ole death will come
Sorrow to many but joy to some
Death is sure but it has no power
Not when Jesus is your strong tower

Be with me on resurrection day
Bound for heaven my new place to stay
May the life you live while here on earth
Be holy and pure like the savior's birth.

The Beauty of a Woman

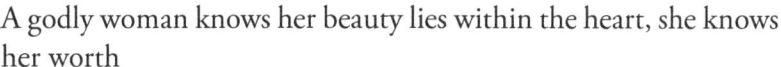

A woman that fears the Lord shall be praised
For she is fearfully, wonderfully, and beautifully made
Her light can shine high upon a dark hill
In her heart lies the beauty of doing God's will

A godly woman knows her beauty lies within the heart, she knows her worth
For God has made her perfectly in time before her birth
Her heart is most delicate when she kneels and pray
God heals her broken heart and wipes her tears away

She is most radiant when she humbles herself before God's throne
Praising Him and worshipping Him when she feels all alone
Her faith can move mountains when God looks at her heart
Giving up is not an option when prayer takes a part

A confident woman can be opinionated, oftentimes speaking her mind
Yet she is compassionate loving and gracefully kind
The beauty of a woman is her mindset that's steadfast on the Lord
Trusting and believing in Him when life seems so hard

In her beauty that lies within comes wisdom and age
She is the salt of the earth wise judicious and her advice is sage
A godly woman is as fair as a rose, yet her beauty lies within
Standing in God's purpose, virtuous before all men.

God Watches

Heaven looks so far away
Wondering will I make it one day

The sun the stars the moon will shine
Will God keep this soul of mine?

This wretched world the miracles it has seen
Surely it knows of sinners redeemed

A new born baby cry at birth
While someone else will leave this earth

The trees bow down to an all wise God
Will a child learn if you spare the rod?

Will a man learn to forgive his brother?
God has said we must love one another

All things happen for a purpose or reason
No one knows when it their season

Right or wrong consequences will follow
Today is the day don't think of tomorrow

What can we do or just take a stand?
God watches the world; it is in His hands.

Women of Excellence

Women of excellence be empowered be strong in the Lord
You can do all things with Him nothing is hard
Be not wavery or doubtful nor be enticed
Be of one mind in the Gospel of Jesus Christ

Women of God be not quarrelsome bring peace into light
We are all precious in God's sight
Stand up everywhere be bold in the word
As missionaries and teachers or ministers let your voice be heard

Women of God be hopeful and encouraging build up not tear down
It is the will of Satan to keep us all bound
Women of excellence be an inspiration let your life be true
Set an example for young women following behind you

Show yourself friendly willing to help others
Lend a helping hand to your sisters and brothers
Make your home a spiritual refuge and prayer your stronghold
You are fighting a spiritual warfare let Satan have no control

Operate in faith, believe in what God can do
Rely on the Holy Spirit he will carry you through
Women of excellence carry the message Jesus is alive
Be compassionate and kind and let love abide.

Making History

People of color are making history now
As in the days of old
In medicine sports education
And even in picture shows

We are still fighting for equal rights
And the injustice in this land
We as people of color
Must all take a stand

Walking in the footsteps of our ancestors
Not feeling their hurt and pain
Their loss of life and bloodshed
Today we count it our gain

Rosa Parks was tired and weary
And she wouldn't give up her bus seat
We must follow in her lead
And do not accept defeat

Martin Luther King had a dream
As he fought for the oppressed
He saw a vision on the mountain top
In the mist of civil unrest

Muhammad Ali, a boxing great,
Stood up for his religious rights
He went to jail but still excelled
In three world championship fights

James Weldon Johnson an educator
Knew what beautiful words could bring
He wrote the Negro National Anthem
Lift every voice and sing

Barack Hussein Obama thought
The world needed a change
He took to the streets of America
In a historic election campaign

Maya Angelou, a poet in modern day,
The author of *Still I Rise*,
What will your story in history be?
Will it be toward the prize

Mother

Mother is that you helping me again
Mother I can remember from way back when
The dirty nose that you wiped so clean
The stern punishment when I was mean

The encouragement you gave here and there
It lets me know how much you care
You were a comfort to me when things fell apart
With love and understanding straight from the heart

Your warm smile and gentle touch
Mother I love you ever so much
You are always giving always praying and doing what needs to be done
Taking care of me since my life begun

I am now older with children of my own
Mother your love still lingers on
The ties that bind us one to another
Is a gift from God, the love of a mother?

God's Eye

A little sparrow fell from a tree
God caught it in his hand
He lifted it up to a higher place
Far from the harms of man

We seek to find the answers
Amid our hurt and pain
We pray and ask God why
Why so much rain

In each life, some rain must fall
But God takes care of his own
God watches as we live out our lives
And then he brings us home.

When I Get Home

All my clothes are packed folded nice and neat
I got my hair done for my going home retreat

I've made the preparations for all the things I'll need
I only thought of myself and of my selfish deeds

Then I thought about my soul had I prepared for it too
All the things I should have done I neglected to do

My soul is not prepared I left it all alone
What will I do when I get home

I had pushed love aside and set faith upon a shelf
I forgot about believing except for in myself

I searched my heart for hope, but it was all gone
What will I do when I get home?

I went to get charity for it was lying about
Then I remembered I had thrown it out

My soul is not prepared I left it all alone
What will I do when I get home

I tried to find patience but it wasn't there
I didn't have much and I really didn't care

Forgiveness was reaching out to me but I pushed it far away
I was holding on to grudges I had from yesterday

My soul is not prepared I left it all alone
What will I do when I get home

Joy oh joy it could not be found
I was living in misery with my head hung down

A knock came to my door a knock of great demand
There stood grace with mercy in its hand

They brought along happiness and peace of mind
And the joy oh joy that I could not find

There was salvation as free as it could be
It was all there all there for me

I grabbed hold of faith and hope was hanging on
And all the other blessings I needed to get home

At last I am packed, I'm ready to go home
My soul is prepared, for I'm not going alone.

Winter

It's a cold wintry morning when snow has blanketed the ground
While sitting at my window listening for a sound

Birds are hardly singing, in the winter's calm
Nestled in their nest with no cause for alarm

Sitting in my easy chair sipping my hot lemon tea
The trees are all bowed down as far as I can see

Mother nature is painting a picture, with her snow and icy mix
She covers the houses, grass and trees and even the little sticks

She covers the rugged mountains, up to their highest peak
It covers the lowly cabin in the woods, where someone lay asleep

The cardinals flying here and there searching for a meal
Children are joyfully playing as they ride their sleds downhill

Winter seem harsh to some folks, some say it is cold and mean
Winter is one of the four seasons that keep the earth beautiful and clean.

Black Man Slave

Look up, black man, look up
That ole slave ship is coming
Look there on the water
Storm clouds are raging billows turning

You were captured to be in bondage
For a season you will be a slave
Work your way to freedom
Not to a pauper's grave

Run, black man, run
One day, you'll be free
Look black man look
The face you see is me

Reach, black man, reach
Grab hold of my hand
I'm here in the sea
And I'm standing on the land

Hold firmly to my hand
I will set you free
Break those chains loosen those ropes
You belong to me

Cast your eyes on the sacred prize
Don't give up the fight
Move swiftly in the moonlit darkness
I'll be your guiding light

Look face-to-face, and eye-to-eye
Let every slave take a stand
Let no fear or despair be in your weary souls
Your freedom is at hand

Teach the young, remind the old
Tell the story of yonder's land
Sing of hope, pray for deliverance
Freedom will be yours, black man

Shout it to the hills, tell it to the mountains
That the ransom for freedom is paid
Cast your eyes toward the heavenly skies
For he's no longer in the grave.

To Love Again

If love ever find you again
Embrace it ever so true
For the love that is within my heart
Is there just for you

When your heart longs for love
And your emotions have gone astray
It is when I think of you my love
In a most special way

The loneliness and sadness can make
The heart ache with pain
Yet deep within my heart
I know I will love again

Love can say in so many words
What the heart longs to hear
Love is in your open arms
That draws me ever so near

Your love can heal my broken heart
By the gentleness of your touch
The warmth of your love my dear
Makes me love you so very much

If love ever finds you again
Be as true to it as you can
For the love that is within my heart
Belongs to such a wonderful man.

The Spirit of Christmas

Christmas is the season for
A special kind of cheer
When families and loved one's gather
With the ones they hold dear

As we sit around the Christmas tree
With sparkling colorful lights
The stars in the sky are rejoicing
And dancing in the night

For in the little town of Bethlehem
The shepherds watched their sheep
The little lambs are watching the stars
For they could not fall asleep

There were three wise men
Traveling from afar
Guided by the brightest
And dancing little star

Hark ole herald the angels were singing
And some blew their horn
Singing go tell the mountains
That a King would soon be born

A man and his wife stopped to an inn
For a place to stay
They were told it was full
Go sleep where the animals lay

They went to a lowly stable
They went without delay
Their little baby boy was born
In a manger filled with hay

Come and see all you faithful
A king has been proclaimed
Born in a lowly manger
Jesus would be his name

It was a holy and silent night
When the world would be redeemed
The angels rejoiced crying
Joy to the earth, for the world has a King.

Divine Mother

Of all the people in the fullness of earth
None so precious as a mother giving birth
By the hands of God a mother was made
By the grace of God her foundation was laid

A mother will be a mother the longest day she lives
In all her days she gives and gives
God protects a mother his faithful dove
He fills her soul with joy and love

A mother will teach her children each day
In the midnight hour she kneels and pray
She prays for her children with shedding tears
That God will keep them through the years

He makes her heart of divine pure gold
A mother's love is everlasting and will never get old
Driven by her faith and compassion for others
The beauty in the spirit of a divine mother.

Life's Blessings

May God's love covers you like the morning dew covers the grass
May His sunlight warm your soul each day that comes to pass

May He rain down blessings on all your hopes and dreams
May He comfort all your pain like the waters of a quiet stream

May His healing pierce your body from your head to your feet
May His heavenly angels protect you every hour of the day of the week

May your life be as bountiful as the sands by the sea
May you live under the shadow of God in perfect harmony.

The Struggle Continues

In the early days of the African slaves, messages were sent through songs
Guiding the runaways to safety to keep them from harm
The work sometimes hard, and the days seem very long
In their hearts were the words of a prayer sung as a song

In the struggling days of yesterday
We think of the ones who paved the way
From field to field some backs were bent
To protesting in streets by the hundreds they went

In times of struggles and unbearable despair
They would bend their knees in a solemn prayer
They sacrificed and died for the lives of many
For fair treatment and justice in this land of plenty

Some progress was made, but the struggle lives on
In hopes of one day, the injustice will be gone
A prayer for one a prayer for each other
A prayer for all the sisters and brothers.

Don't You Know

Come to me, my little child,
And tell me why you cry
Don't you know this world of sinners
Is the reason I had to die?

Come to me, my little child,
And tell me why you hide
Don't you know that I can see?
I can see you from every side

Come to me, my little child,
And tell me what you fear
Don't you know you're never alone?
That I am always near

Come to me, my little child,
And tell me why you are in pain
Don't you know that I'm a healer?
It is for you that I was slain

Come to me, my little child,
And tell me why you are lost
Don't you know that I am your savior?
And for your sins I paid the cost

Come to me, my little child,
And tell me why you are redeemed
Don't you know whose child you are?
You are the child of the King.

A Mother's Love

A mother's love is purer than gold
A mother's love will God behold
A mother's love is always there
Even when life is hard to bear

A mother's love will calm a child's fear
With hugs and kisses and holding him near
A mother will teach her child to behave
To love, to respect, to share always

A mother's work will last all day
And into the night when she kneels to pray
A mother will guide her children through the years
When life gets hard and full of tears

A mother will keep her house a home
Even when her children are grown and gone
As time goes on, a mother will get old
Still her love will God behold.

When Not to Pray

When there is no pain or tears to shed
Or no more sickness on death beds

When peace like a river your soul at rest
When there on earth you've done your best

When trials and tribulations cease to be
When the glory of God is all you see

When you can walk around heaven all day
Is when you don't have to pray

Or
When your soul is tormented in the flames
It's too late to call on His name

When praying was just a bother to you
And you did just what you wanted to do

You had no time to spend with God
You were busy on the wide road you trod

When hell's gates open wide
Don't be surprise to see whose inside

All because you would not pray
Or confess to God that you wanted to be saved.

O Merciful God (Prayer)

As I sit here thinking all about my life
How God has brought me through it in joy, sorrow, and strife

It takes but a moment to bow my head and pray
As I go about my duties of each new dawning day

Sometimes I take for granted the things I do and say
I forget that God has brought me out of a horrible pit
And out of the miry clay

Hear my prayer, Lord, and give ear unto my cry
For I will trust in you, Lord, till the day I die

God reigns over the heavens He sits upon his throne
He waits for day of judgement when He brings his people home

Wash me, O Lord, from my iniquity and cleanse me from my sins
Straighten out my heart, dear God, and let thy grace grow deep within

Deliver me from the workers of iniquity and save me from bloody men
For woe they lie in wait for my soul as I silently say amen.

Retirement

How do you say goodbye to a family you've
worked with for years?
How do you walk away when eyes are
filled with tears?

Moving on to the next chapter in your life
wondering what you will do
knowing you have to keep busy
and what interest will you pursue

Reminiscing back on your job, how the
faces of your coworkers looked
their laughs, their corny jokes, their ups
and downs, and the pictures that you took

You're wondering if they will remember you
as the days and years go by
what if you passed them on the streets
and they didn't tell you hi.

The people that we meet in life maybe
there just for a season
some will stay for lasting friendships
others will leave for no apparent reason

It is good to be nice to people as
we live from day to day
we may never see them again
no one comes here to stay.

Coming of Age

Sitting in a rest home waiting room
Patients all around,
Some are broken hearted,
Others are weary and down;

Most are old and feeble
Their bodies ache with pain,
Their faces drawn with wrinkles,
No youth left to regain;

Their thoughts are reminiscing,
To the days of long ago,
Their steps have decreased
To a pace that's humble and slow;

Some are young at heart,
Their minds sharp and keen,
Mentally alert,
With plenty of self-esteem;

Yet they are fragile,
Most often they are used,
Left alone in agony,
Mistreated and abused;

They possess experience and wisdom,
Which helps young minds to grow,
If we take care of the elderly,
Knowledge this world will know.

Happy Thoughts

Happiness is awakening to a morning that
you've never seen,
Happiness is a beautiful day,
the sun shining with gleam.

Happiness is a cheerful child,
no worries, hunger, or fear,
Happiness is a caring person,
who loves that child so dear.

Happiness is a free country,
where everyone has his say,
Happiness is the land,
where peace is longing to stay.

Happiness is a marriage,
and with work it will last,
Happiness is looking to the future,
and not rekindling the past.

Happiness is being healthy,
our bodies feeling at ease,
Happiness is longevity,
if we rid the world of disease.

Happiness is no starvation,
and there's a lot in this world,
Happiness is feeding,
all the poor little boys and girls.

Happiness is love,
that what this world really needs,
Happiness is charity,
and doing someone a good deed.

Happiness is in Jesus,
our savior, guide, and friend,
Happiness is knowing,
He'll stand by you to the end.

Happiness is happiness,
what else can it be,
If we live and die in Christ,
our souls will surely be free.

No Rocks Cry Out for Me

When peace like a river flow
In His hands my life He holds
No rocks cry out for me

When storms are raging about me still
And I press my way to do His will
No rocks cry out for me

When my hands are raised to the heavenly sky
And my feet dance to a joyous high
No rocks cry out for me

When I lift my voice in a worshiping praise
I promise to serve Him all my days
No rocks cry out for me

When my head and knees bow before the throne of grace
I have strength to run this Christian race
No rocks cry out for me

The service I give is to His glory
I'm a servant of God, I tell His story
No rocks cry out for me

When my faith shines bright before truths unseen
I exalt His name for souls redeemed
No rocks cry out for me

Staying on my post, I watch and pray
For He will come again someday
No rocks cry out for me

When I have said what He told me to say
And the world blindly goes its way
No rocks cry out for me

When there is nothing left for me to do
I will stand before God, me and you
No rocks will cry out for me.

Fall of Man

When man comes to the end of the road
He's no longer young, he's growing old
A man who lead such a life so grand
Ever since God first made man

When he drew his first breath of life
God knew he'd be lonely, God gave him a wife
God put the man in a deep, deep sleep
Not a sound was heard from the animals that creeped

He took from the man one great rib
God has made another life which would forever live
The man name was Adam the woman Eve
From the Garden of Eden they could not leave

When they ate of the fruit from the forbidden tree
From the Garden they thought we must flee
Now they will face an earthly death
For the sin they had done and the Garden they left

They went out into the world to make a new life
They had many hardships and many strife
When man comes to the end of the road
Death will come to both young and old.

And They Called Him Jesus

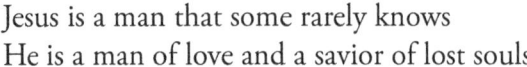

Jesus is a man that some rarely knows
He is a man of love and a savior of lost souls

Believe in him trust in him obey him that you may
He will lead you and guide you in the right way

Pray to him talk to him tell him your every woe
His words will always comfort you and his peace you will know

Witness for him testify of him don't be ashamed
Praise him serve him magnify his holy name

Read about him learn about him seek out all that you can
Faith is what you really need to be with this glorious man

Salvation is there for you, and he gave it to us free
Cast your cares upon him and be what he'll have you to be

He's worthy, he's worthy more times than you can say
Glory, glory hallelujah we'll be with him someday.

Finding Your Way

When your present remembers your past
And you are trying to come home
Are you looking for that moment in time?
That you thought was surely gone

Are you searching for something?
That you hoped was still there
And you can't seem to find it
No, not anywhere

When you remember that divine love
And your faith was so intense
Striving towards a call
For a Godly recompense

Your heart is searching for something
That your soul once knew
That divine presence of God
As you sat on the church pew

In secret and in silence
The prayers and tears flowed
You were broken and sad
Your spirit humbled and low

Look inside your heart
Because God's love runs deep
God's love is everlasting
Is that what you seek?

When your present remembers your past
It may be better than some
Then you can see where grace and mercy
Has brought you from

God is omnipresent
For you are not alone
Wherever you may be
God's love will bring you home.

About the Author

Linda Glasper King has been writing poetry for a number of years. She has written poetry for church programs, funeral programs, and poetry tributes for pastors and retirees' celebrations.

She has received diplomas from the Institute of Children Literature for creating and selling short stories and articles as well as for writing for children and teenagers.

Linda has also attained the distinction, distinguished member with all the privileges accorded thereto, and is recognized for support of the society's principles of peace education–accomplishment–charity–equality from the International Society of Poets.

A retired US postal employee, Linda resides in Raleigh, North Carolina, with her three children and eight grandchildren.

CPSIA information can be obtained
at www.ICGtesting.com
Printed in the USA
BVHW031409160919
558565BV00006B/74/P